Praise f(
The Ric

"*Jamil Frazier has set a new standard for what is possible in life. I have watched him break free from the shackles of his past to create immense success, not only for him, but for anyone who wants it. If you want to have more, do more, and be more, this book is for you, because Jamil gives you everything you need in a simple, concise way. Prepare yourself for growth and success as you follow the footsteps of someone who's truly done the work!*"

Karen Ellstrom, *entrepreneur and business leader*

THE
RICHEST
MAN
IN DIRECT SALES

Jamil Frazier

Copyright © 2020 by Jamil Frazier

Published by Think Life Is Different Media

ISBN: 978-1-7344222-4-5

THINK LIFE
is DIFFERENT

Table of Contents

Dedication

Ezra, Mila & Cruz – I dedicate this book to you. Your mother and I love you more than you know. I wrote this book (and all the others) with you in mind. My hope and prayer is that they are read and passed down for generations to come in the Frazier family.

CHAPTER 1

Echo Income

If you're measuring bank accounts, I'm not the richest man in direct sales.

But I'm very rich in something else.

While I don't know for sure who the richest person is, we have something in common, far more important than checkbook balances: we found the system that works.

The system, not *a* system.

Over the past seven years, I have figured out how to generate wealth, going from nail-biting about trying to pay bills with nickels and dimes, to where I am now, complete financial independence. And that's the wealth, that's what makes me rich.

It's the assurance of not only having money today, but being able to generate that income from here on out.

I call it "echo income."

Just like your voice reverberates down a canyon, your income can echo, coming back again and again when you find the right system, one where your product or service adds constant value that your customers or clients are happy to pay for on an ongoing basis.

This kind of wealth earns you independence, which is a richness beyond money. Here is what independence has looked like for me:

♦   Complete flexibility, so I can do what I want when I want to

♦   Enjoying world-class experiences anywhere in the world

♦   A thriving marriage instead of a failing marriage

♦   Deep relationships with others, especially my children

♦   Peace and comfort in my own mind

♦   Time to teach these principles to tens-of-thousands

♦   Opportunity to date myself and understand who I really am

♦   And the greatest wealth of all, an ability to give generously to the causes I believe in.

A rich man is one whose children run into his arms, even though his hands are empty. And this is the kind of life *and independence* we can truly build. This book will share with you the principles I have used to find independence, and I am still using today to gain even more.

What Is Financial Independence?

Financial independence is when you no longer have to work to pay your bills.

Your outputs are divorced from your inputs. Rather than being compensated for hours spent, you're compensated for long-term value added.

When your business revenue, investments and your cash flow exceed your monthly expenses without you having to show up to work every day all day, you have financial independence. When you work not because you have to, but because you want to, you have financial independence.

What's the price tag on financial independence?

How much is it worth to build up a business that brings in echo income that covers what I need in a month, and then some?

What is the value of knowing I could stop working today, and not worry about whether or not there'd be money to pay bills tomorrow, that the money would still flow in from what I've already set up?

Financial independence is about peace of mind, and there is no price tag on that.

It is wealth beyond belief.

From Falling Apart To Freedom

This wasn't always the case. Direct sales wasn't something I knew much about at all.

After college, I worked in pharmaceutical sales and medical equipment sales, and I even worked full-time as a medical consultant.

I wanted something more. I wanted more opportunity. I wanted income that flowed in whether I was constantly making new sales or not, though the closest I'd come to such a thing was basic investing and dabbling in purchasing patents.

I won't lie and say I jumped at the chance to be in direct sales. Instead, in 2012, direct sales found me. Things in my life were falling apart; relationships, physical health, and stress were all taking their toll.

My weight had burgeoned, and I was disgusted at where I'd ended up. I knew I needed to make some changes, so I found a health program and a coach to help me get my physical health back on track.

Physical health impacts so much in life, far more than just the body, as I discovered after a few weeks of getting healthy. I was feeling great, with high energy and confidence and a renewed excitement for life. It had been so long since I was happy and had even liked myself.

You can bet that people notice that kind of change. My family and friends saw the difference in me, and recognized they needed the same thing in their life. It wasn't long before I had the chance to coach others using the same health program, just as I'd been coached, as an independent business owner.

At first I thought of this as my side business, something extra besides my "real" job, not realizing the path opening up before me. A few months later, I had the opportunity to attend a conference in Washington, D.C. where I met others who were just like me. They were building amazing businesses, helping other people make their lives better, controlling their own time—all while earning incredible incomes.

The potential for financial independence was breathtaking, but so was the trickle-down effect in their lives. Some told me how their marriages would have failed had they not decided to go after a life of freedom. Others shared the positive changes in their physical and mental health.

I was hooked.

Everything I was hearing was exactly what I wanted not only for myself, but for the lives I could potentially change for the better. I could envision people who were in the same trap I'd been in, and being given the opportunity to exchange that for health and happiness. I also saw that I had an opportunity to help my family and build wealth and security for all of us.

To do that, though, I needed to come to a crossroads. I couldn't serve two masters, and so, just a few months later, I left my "real" consulting job and took a full leap into direct sales. Splitting my time between the two was no longer working, and I knew I needed to commit to making the direct sales path really work.

To make it really work, I really worked. In just ten months after committing full time to direct sales, my business was in the top one percent in the industry in the country. By year five, my business started doing over ten million dollars in revenue a year.[1]

---

[1] Please understand, in no way am I making specific income or revenue promises. Your situation is unique, as is mine. While I believe in these principles wholeheartedly, they are no guarantee to income.

It was at that point I realized that there are two kinds of money problems: not having enough, and having more than you needed.

The Importance Of Financial Intelligence

Maybe you're like me years ago, when I would never have believed a person could have too much money. It sounds crazy, doesn't it?

While having more than you need of something is morally neutral (neither good nor bad), it can bring challenges and responsibilities. You have to be willing to meet them. This is the difference between controlling your money or letting it control you.

Financial intelligence is something that is lacking in both my industry specifically, but also across the country. I've worked with thousands of people, mentoring them as they start their own business, and have seen this reality firsthand.

I noticed that, for the most part, people who start with direct sales have similar desires, just like I did. They want to help others change their lives for the better, and they want to improve their own lives. In fact, nearly every person I worked with wanted the same things, whether it was more time, more money, a larger purpose, or less stress.

Can you blame them? Don't we all want more control over our time and financial independence? Who doesn't like the idea of echo income, where the money regularly comes in without having to fight for each dollar?

But there was a significant problem, and it's the very reason I wrote this book: the opportunity to make the money was there, but because they did not know how to handle their finances, they never built wealth. Money came in, and then it went out. Spending increased. Instead of accumulating assets, they accumulated liabilities in both their business and personal finances.

Instead of financial independence, they were still stuck in the rat race they had so desperately wanted to get out of. They might have been working for themselves and owned a business, but the reality was the business owned them and they were still financial prisoners.

CHAPTER 2

The Richest Man In Babylon

W ho knew personal development mattered when the money was coming in?

My mentor had suggested that I look into personal development, something I knew very little about. I had no idea what she meant, but she'd recommended that I watch a man named Jim Rohn. I found Rohn, and during one of his talks, zeroed in on a book he mentioned, *The Richest Man In Babylon* by George Clason.

"Even though buying, reading, and studying this book is easy to do and can completely change your life, I know only a few of you will read it," Rohn said. What he said challenged me, and I ordered that book before Rohn was even finished with his talk.

You see, at that point in my life, I was in the uncomfortable place many of you are in, where you have lots of ambition and lots of ideas, but very little knowledge about financial matters. You want to increase your wealth, but don't have a plan for when it happens. This problem was personally made real when someone came to me soon after I had listened to Rohn.

"Jamil," he'd asked me, "if I were to travel around the country and give seminars on what a good financial plan should look like, would you feel comfortable if I used your plan to inspire them?"

There was no way I wanted him to do that! My financial plan was barely existent, and what I did have was horrible. I was embarrassed by the state of things, because by that point in my life, with all I had been through and accomplished, I ought to have created a real plan.

It was the intersection of these two incidents that made me realize I needed a new paradigm. Clason's book was crucial in accomplishing that, and for the rest of this book, I'm going to show you how to put his system to work, the same way I put it to work for me. We'll go over Clason's five laws and seven cures specific to direct sales businesses.

Because, once I began following them, I became financially independent in just five and a half years.[2]

---

[2] These results were true for me in my context and situation. Please understand, this should not be taken as a promise or guarantee of the same results. However, the principles are sound and will serve you well—regardless of your individual results.

CHAPTER 3
Pay Yourself First

Clason's First Law:
Start Thy Purse To Fattening

"Gold cometh gladly and increasing quantity to any man who will put not less than one-tenth of his earnings to create an estate for his future and that of his family."

– George Clason

You have to pay yourself first.

I'm not kidding. Stop being okay with paying everyone else and start being okay paying yourself first.

It seems like an obvious approach to building wealth, but the reality is that most people pay someone else first. When I was working for others, my paycheck had taxes taken out by the government. So I paid the government. Then I paid rent. So I paid my landlord. Then I paid my bills. So I paid Verizon, Edison, Toyota, the wine club I had no business being a part of, and all these other companies and people.

On the rare occasion that something was left over (and it was rare indeed), I would limp to the bank to put whatever small amount I had into a savings account. I wasn't building much wealth at all, and often felt like I was always behind the curve financially, no matter how much my income increased.

That order is completely backwards.

As Clason says, the first thing I needed to do when I received money was to pay myself. For every dollar I earned, according to Clason, no less than ten percent would immediately be saved. After I'd paid myself in this way, I could pay other bills.

My personal approach to this method was to start paying myself thirty percent of everything I earned each month, with ten percent to savings, ten percent towards investments, and ten percent to charity or tithing.

This was non-negotiable. There was no situation or excuse where I would allow myself to do anything else. No one got my money before I took my portion out first.

It didn't matter how much or how little I earned; the first payment always went to me. This way, I stayed ahead of the curve, and learned to live on seventy percent of my income.

No one builds wealth living paycheck to paycheck, yet that unquestioned mindset is what most people do when they don't pay themselves first. We have accepted that others get the money we earned before we do. We hand over the money that should go to our families and our futures.

The first law completely changed how I thought about my money and the money my business made.

When your money comes in, pay yourself first.

CHAPTER 4

Live Below Your Means

Clason's Second Law:
Control Thy Expenditures

"Confuse not the necessary expenses with thy desires."

– George Clason

It doesn't do you any good if you pay yourself first and then live above the remaining means.

In my business and personal finances, I had to learn to "lean" our spending habits. Since I was paying myself thirty percent instead of the minimal ten percent that Clason recommended, I had to train myself to live off of seventy percent of my income instead of one hundred percent.

There's nothing easy about reducing your expenses and learning to live on less. To make this happen for my finances, I had to take into account two of the most important things I've learned over the years, two of the most difficult concepts for people to exercise: emotional intelligence and delayed gratification.

The Two Most Difficult Concepts You Must Grasp

Emotional intelligence is the ability to be aware of and control your emotions. Delayed gratification simply means you're able to put off the satisfaction of an immediate reward, and wait for a later reward.

Spending money is an emotional thing. We use it to buy things or experiences that answer emotional needs. You will never decrease your expenses if you lack emotional intelligence and delayed gratification. Ironically these are the very things you will need to build a massive direct sales business, too.

Take a look around your house. How much of what you've purchased do you even want or use? Believe me, I know what it feels like. I was there too, and as I was grappling with Clason's second law, it dawned on me how much I had purchased and how little of it I actually used.

I could see Pareto's Principle clearly at work in my life. This principle states that about eighty percent of the effects or results we see come from twenty percent of the causes or activity, and vice versa.

I realized that twenty percent of the clothes in my closet I wore eighty percent of the time, so I gave away or sold eighty percent of the clothes I wore only twenty percent of the time. Twenty percent of the CDs in my car I listened to eighty percent of the time, so I gave away or sold eighty percent of CDs that I only listened to twenty percent of the time.

For most people, an increase in income means an increase in spending.

You get a raise on the job, and you buy a new car or things you don't need. You get a bonus and you feel you need to reward yourself by spending it.

When you raise your expenses to match your income, you've canceled any wealth-building benefits.

Even when I was making nearly $20,000 a month[3], I chose to live far below those means and remain in a small, rented condo.

Even when we did move to a new home, we kept our expenses in mind and chose a smaller home in a less expensive neighborhood. We kept our old vehicles and put our extra money into investment rental properties that had immediate cash flow.

---

[3] This principle is true regardless of your income level. Living below your means creates a surplus each month.

What was the key here?

If you're going to master the second law, you need to differentiate between "need" and "want."

I didn't need a big house, new cars or fancy vacations. They would have been nice, but I chose to delay that gratification with an eye on getting control of my finances and becoming financially independent. It wasn't easy watching friends purchase big beautiful houses, new cars, and sporting Rolex watches, but I had to practice emotional intelligence and not let feelings dictate how I spent my money.

There was one prize for me, and that was to fatten three purses: savings, investing, and tithing.

"In due time," I often told myself when I saw others spending money. "In due time. Do it the right way."

The more controlled and leaner our spending became, the more I refused to spend any money on something we didn't need, and the more my income increased—it wasn't long before I shifted from paying myself thirty percent and bumped it up to forty percent.

We lived off of only sixty percent of our income and our wealth continued to grow.

For any of this to work, you will need to set a budget or many budgets. That was new to me at the time, but in order to control spending, both personal and business budgets were necessary.

At the start, when I was paying myself thirty percent of every dollar I earned, I had to create a budget that fit living expenses into seventy percent of my income. And, once I created those budgets, I had to stick with them.

Most people can grasp the need for a personal finance budget, but it's trickier when it comes to their business. A business budget might seem less important because it's easy to assume every expense will be a tax write-off, when in reality, it's a justification for excess spending.

"I can travel, eat out, or buy promotional items as much as I want because I can write it off," you might think.

In my direct selling business, leanness was still necessary.

I couldn't compartmentalize. This was an overall rehabilitation of how I approached money, and I needed to put it to work in every area of finances. There must be consistency for the habit to take root and for the wealth-building benefits to reach into all areas, personal and business.

Remember how I looked around my home and saw Pareto's Principle at work as I tried to get control of personal spending?

I saw Pareto's Principle in my business as well, where twenty percent of my business partners produced eighty percent of the revenue, and eighty percent of the business partners were only responsible for twenty percent. To grow my business, I began spending and investing eighty percent of my mentoring and leadership development with the twenty percent of people who were highly motivated, leaving only twenty percent of my time for the eighty percent who were less motivated.

CHAPTER 5

Make Your Money Work For You

Clason's Third Law—
Make Thy Gold Multiply

"Gold clingeth to the protection of the cautious owner who invests it under the advice of men wise in its handling."

– George Clason

Even God wants our money to work for us.
As a boy, I learned of the story in Matthew 25 in which a wise and wealthy master is about to leave his household to do some traveling. Before he leaves, he gathers three of his servants to him and asks them to take care of his gold. One servant receives five pieces. Another servant receives two pieces. The last servant receives just one piece of gold. The master tells them that, when he returns, he wants to see his money multiplied.

After a time, the master returns. He calls the three servants to him to see what they've done with his money. The first two reported that they put his money to work and had doubled what he'd given them. The master was pleased. The third servant, however, reported that he hadn't done anything with the master's money. Out of fear, he had chosen to bury it in the ground and hide it.

The master was extremely disappointed.

I'm not joking about the extreme nature of his disappointment. The master took the money from the third servant, called him wicked and lazy, and had him thrown outside into the "outer darkness, where there will be weeping and gnashing of teeth."

Wow.

When I heard that story as a boy, I remember thinking, even back then, that God wants our money to work for us, and that we have a role to play in that. There are expectations for us.

Here's the best part, though. The master gave that lazy servant's gold to the servant who had turned five pieces of gold into ten. "For the one who has will be given more, and he will have more than enough. But the one who does not have, even what he has will be taken from him."

Don't we see this at work in the world today? Don't we hear of how the "rich get richer and the poor get poorer"? In reading about wealth growth, I came across a statement that said if we were to take all the money away from the wealthiest five percent of the people in this country, they'd have it back in their hands in just a few years.

It's about financial intelligence, it's about having the right spending habits, it's about being focused on wealth building, it's about the mindset ... and it's about investing.

The wealthy spend their time buying assets, while the poor and middle class spend their time buying "things." I wanted to be wealthy.

A Solid Philosophy For Investing

Once you have the habit of paying yourself first, it's not enough to just bury your ten percent in a low-yield savings account. You'll need to find some investments to make your money work for you.

This is where the fun and frustration merged in my wealth-building journey. There are so many different ideas, philosophies, strategies, resources, and people who will tell you completely opposing methods to take when investing. You will rarely find agreement on any one particular investment approach.

I made a lot of investment mistakes at first. My advisors had told me not to run my business as a sole proprietorship because it got to the point where it was bringing in too much income that would require me to pay too much in taxes. However, I did not listen because I thought I could save a few hundred dollars. Instead, by not establishing a corporation, I nearly lost thousands in taxes. To avoid that, I had to invest in the stock market and mutual funds. 401ks and IRAs. Even though I eventually changed the business entity to a corporation, I used the same investment vehicles.

One of the things to look into are the differences between good and bad assets. Some of the investment models I used in the early days are quite phenomenal—they're just a little bit slower. In some circles, even though those investment models are good, they are also bad (I use the term loosely here).

A bad asset is one that takes a lot of capital, and keeps it for far too long. You don't get a decent return in a timely manner. You will need to decide what a timely manner is for you.

Fast And Slow Assets

While I'm not going to tell you exactly what (or how) you should invest your money in, I want you to understand something about assets that'll help you make informed decisions. Whatever you decide to invest in, know there are fast assets and slow assets. Each type puts money back into your pocket, but one will do it much quicker (and with less of your capital), and the other will do it more slowly (with more of your capital). Regardless of your choice, follow the 10/10/10 strategy: save ten percent, invest ten percent, and give ten percent. I want to encourage you to not get so bogged down on what to invest in like I did. Find a great team of advisors to support you. I also want to let you know, and I have found this to be true for myself: Once you have your investment bucket filled up, the right opportunities, people, and returns tend to find you. That is a secret they don't teach in schools. The more you have to invest, the more access is granted, the better deals (in real estate, businesses or mutual funds) are opened up to you, and the possibilities for better returns. This is one of the ways the rich get richer.

Now, once you start investing, and money starts coming in, remember: pay yourself at least ten percent first! Again, I'm not going to tell you which investment you should make, or who you should work with. That's beyond the scope of this book. However, here are two key areas I will be so bold as to tell you to invest in, and are perfectly in line with Clason's recommendation:

- ◆   Invest in your own business.
- ◆   Invest in your own people.

What investment could you possibly know better than those two?

Invest In Your Business

I can tell you with certainty that you ought to be investing back into your own business no matter how big or small it is. By not doing so, you're telling that Higher Power (or whatever you'd like to call it) that you aren't all that serious about your business and that it's open season on having it taken from you.

In fact, I consider this one of the biggest mistakes small business owners make. In all my years of mentoring, I've seen this enough. Business owners who don't invest back in their business, refusing to use their funds to grow their business or increase their education, fail to be a success. They waste their business income to fund a lifestyle (remember rule number two!) instead of their own business. They bleed the life out of their business instead of feeding life back into it.

I can attest to this truth through my own experience. My direct sales business had only been going for ten months when my mentor suggested that I attend a seminar in Dallas, Texas.

"Are you crazy," I said to her. "That's going to cost one thousand dollars!"

"No, young grasshopper," she said, "that's going to be an investment back into your business of one thousand dollars where you will see a massive return if you use and follow the principles you'll learn."

I didn't stop with Dallas. Soon I was traveling to San Diego, Salt Lake City, Nashville, Tucson, Los Angeles, and more. In the next ten months, my income doubled, and then doubled again!

If you have a mentor, ask them where they invest their money. (And if you don't have a mentor ... get one ASAP!)

And remember that, to be blunt, if you don't invest back in your own business, it's like business suicide.

Invest In Your People

Not only do you want to invest in your own business, but you want to invest back into your own people. Use part of your capital to thank, inspire, motivate, incentivize, and reward. One of the best returns you will ever get on your money is making your customers, clients, and team feel valued and appreciated.

I've taken a variety of approaches to this, because it often depends on the team members. Perhaps you'll give them a gift card, a weekend getaway, team dinners, flowers, or even baby diapers! Seemingly small things go a long way to let people know they are valued.

Investing in other people and encouraging them is never a bad investment. In fact, we're going to cover one more such investment in greater detail in Chapter 9. You won't want to skip it.

CHAPTER 6

Do Not Lose Money

Clason's Fourth Law—
Guard Thy Treasures From Loss

"Gold slippeth away from the man who invests it in businesses or purposes with which he is not familiar or which are not approved by those skilled in its keep."

– George Clason

You must invest only in what you understand. This is one of the primary things I've done differently.

I spent hours studying up on mutual funds and the stock market. Clason says in his book that you ought to invest in things you know. I'll cover this in more detail in the next chapter, but my own personal experience in investing bears it out.

I found investing almost too confusing at first, but I have since learned to only invest in things, people, businesses and markets that make sense to me. It seems obvious, but before I got to this point, I was too scared to ask others for an explanation. I didn't want to look stupid. I cared too much about what other people thought, and because of that I lost a lot of money.

Today, I do not move forward if it doesn't make sense.

One of the quickest routes to losing money is to hand it over to someone who can't even explain in a way that you can understand how they are going to make your money grow.

Today, my simple approach to business has paid off.

Your Business Is Like The Seasons

Over the first few years of building my business and wealth, I discovered that my industry and investing worked much like the seasons in nature. There is a spring, summer, fall, and winter.

Remember, your business is your greatest asset. Especially when you build it the right way. It's the "treasure" that Clason is talking about in his fourth law. As with any industry, there is a time for great life, great harvest, great production, and great action.

Some months fly by and feel like everything is clicking. It seems as if everything you touch turns to gold and you can do no wrong. I call those times the seasons of spring and summer, where your investments and business are growing and Murphy's Law doesn't seem to exist.

But spring and summer don't stick around.

You will see fall and winter next. You'll have times where the revenue slows down. Business partners and employees leave. Personal issues in your family and life create stress and distraction. The market or economy has an adverse effect on your wealth.

Always Guard Your Work And Wealth

Just remember that if the market is up, it will always come down. If you're having golden times, you will absolutely have some that aren't. And when times are tough, remember that spring and summer are coming. It is all cyclical, so your job is to figure out how to hedge your losses, find safer investments in the lean times, and plan in summer before fall sets in.

Basically, you have to learn how to guard your hard work in spring and summer.

In my early years of building my business, I was naive enough to think that sheer motivation and equally eager members of my team were a guarantee for instant and sustained success. The return was incredible and so I took that as a sign we all knew what we were doing. I was busy planting seeds and watching things grow all spring and summer, but left the results to wither in fall and winter.

It was a disaster! It took almost eight months of extra hard work to bring my organization back to where it had been. I had let all of the hard work go unattended, unguarded, and my crops ended up ruined.

Whatever you build, you must remember to guard with all of your might. Whether it's relationships, business, investments, family—if you leave it too soon, all alone, you'll miss the harvest.

This ties into Clason's rules in that we can't be stupid when it comes to investing.

Are you lending money? Make sure there is significant collateral for your loan. You don't lend money or co-sign a loan for your sister to start a new boutique store without careful thought and real collateral.

As Clason says through the character Arkad in his book, we're to guard our "treasure" from loss by only investing our wealth:

- Where the principal is safe
- Where the principal may be reclaimed if you need to
- Where you will collect a fair rent or return

And, as I mentioned in the previous chapter, Clason says you should only take the financial advice of people who have a history of wise investments and creating profit with the money they invest. However, I'd like to show how your investment bucket can be used to rapidly pay down debt.

How To Rapidly Pay Off Debt

When I started this process we were in piles of debt: student loan debt, credit card debt, automobile debt, and even some debt that had gone to collections. To gain control, I listed every debt on paper, in order of highest to lowest balance and interest rates.

Immediately, I used the 10/10/10 strategy to take the funds we were building in our investment bucket and re-invest them back into debt repayment. There was no better investment than to clear debt from the start.

Debt gnaws at you, so I wanted to be absolutely debt-free. Today, we've stayed that way—outside of our real estate holdings, houses, and rental properties.

The process for clearing our debt was simple. I started with the smallest payment and set up a game plan to pay that off.

One of the smallest was my $500 student loan payment. At that point, I was making the minimum payment of roughly sixty dollars per month. Now that I was paying myself according to the 10/10/10 rule, I added the ten percent investment funds toward that student loan bill. In the beginning, that amount was nominal—but over time it grew and the habit compounded.

Here's a hypothetical snapshot.

Let's say I earned $3,000 that first month. This meant $300 went to savings, $300 to investing, and $300 to giving. I then re-routed the $300 toward debt repayment. This was aligned with my goal to pay off that student loan as fast as possible.

Now I put $360 toward it until it was paid off. That loan was paid off pretty darn fast, which is important because fast wins reinforce new habits. It is also good for your psychological well-being. With every debt gone, you feel a little lighter.

Plus, my hammer to knock down the next debt was now $360 per month.

The next debt was a $1,000 dental payment that I had been paying $100 a month toward. Now I added $360 monthly, taking the total repayment to $460 per month. This means that dental bill would be gone in just three months. And once paid, I had $460 to put towards the next debt.

Next in line was a $5,000 credit card we had also been paying $100 a month towards. We attacked that debt with $560 per month. Meanwhile, I still made minimum payments on all other debt. But this allowed me to clear off this credit card bill in about eight months.

As a final example, we focused on a $6,000 car note that I had been paying $150 a month towards. Adding that to the freed up $560 per month and I had $710 to put towards the $6000 payment. This loan evaporated in just eleven months.

It's important to remember here that I was also building my business while repaying debt using this system. So, as my income grew, so did the ten percent "investment" toward debt repayment. What had started as a $300 monthly debt repayment skyrocketed to $1,000 because I'd tripled my income.

This strategy is how we paid off considerable debt in about two years—and how you can, too.

The crazy thing is that, eventually, I had over $2,500 to pay off debt. Once all of our debts (outside of real estate) were repaid, that $2,500 stayed in my investment bucket. Rather than repaying creditors, I was paying myself today *and* well into the future. We never deviated from the 10/10/10 strategy.

It rapidly clears off debt and installs the habit of investing.

Rather than following some of the financial philosophies of the world down the road of bankruptcy, you're building your own road to fortune. And remember, a wise wallet creates a peaceful mind.

CHAPTER 7

Own Your Home

Clason's Fifth Law—Own Thy Own Home

"To own his own domicile and to have it a place he is proud to care for, putteth confidence in his heart and greater effort behind all his endeavors. Therefore, do I recommend that every man own the roof that sheltereth him and his."

– George Clason

Strive to own your own ship—starting with your house. Almost more important than the house is the land the house sits on.

History teaches that over time property appreciates. In fact, as Clason tells us, the benefits of ownership go even deeper than your bank account. It gives peace and builds a legacy of wealth for your family. This is how the richest of the rich maintain their wealth over generations—they pass down their properties, homes and estates.

The reason I bought our current house was for my children and also their children. It was strategically chosen to become the first piece of their portfolio. And my plan was to grow it from here.

It is also about peace of mind. When you own your own stuff, you don't have to worry about getting thrown out. It's as simple as that.

For example, a couple of years ago, a family member came to me after being thrown out of her house. Her landlord decided it was time to sell and gave her thirty days to move out.

She was in a difficult position, because she had never held down a job and her credit was poor. It's hard to secure another place without income and great credit. She approached my wife and me, and we were able to buy her a house. Now, she has the peace of mind that she will be okay.

It's a noble investment. But spiritually, philosophically, and mentally, it's even more than that.

I Want To Be A Bob

Right now, we're planning on purchasing another property with five acres of land, a vineyard, and rolling hills because I want to walk on earth that I own.

Seven years ago, I couldn't even get a loan to purchase a $250,000 condo. They wouldn't even entertain us. Today, I own multiple properties, rental units, and homes of our own.

How?

When I was in fifth grade, we rented a little house in Temple City, CA. Our landlord was an older man named Bob. When he came by, we always sat up straight, picked up frantically, and made his place look immaculate.

I watched him closely, and honestly, wanted to be a Bob, on the other side of ownership. Not the kid who's sitting up straight prepping for the landlord's arrival. I wanted to be the landlord. I wanted to be the guy who walked with the confidence that he owned the ground beneath his floors.

I was driven to own real estate like Bob.

A Lofty Goal

This is a lofty goal, especially for people starting out in direct sales—or any industry. However, doing this made me realize something profound: *to gain more, I had to become more.*

Set a goal so high you have to grow into the person who can see that realized. Not simply owning your home, but understanding who you have to become to realize it. I did not have anyone who gave us money (or even contributed money) for a downpayment. I did not have anyone to lend money to us. I built it by using the 10/10/10 strategy.

In order to use this strategy over time, you will have to become more, and owning will become a wealth-generating machine.[4]

It's about the plan. There may be many out there. But pick one and follow it. This has become a blueprint for me to follow. In my experience, this has worked for me. Plus, this is how wealth gets transferred (and this even forms the family mind).

Seven years ago, we couldn't even get a loan. Now we can get just about any loan we want. I'm simply sharing what's worked for us. Regardless of your path to ownership, though, your home should be a profitable investment.

Remember my own personal "pay myself first" strategy? I sent ten percent to savings, ten percent to investments, and gave ten percent. By doing this, I was able to build up a nest egg to purchase our first home.

---

[4] Some argue that property ownership *is not* one of the smartest paths to wealth, but that conversation is beyond the scope of this book. I've experienced—and seen first-hand—the financial and mental benefits of owning real estate.

It only took a few years of this practice of paying off debt and building up reserves.

And, by sticking to that plan, we were able to buy two more homes that same year, one of which we wholesaled and another that we kept as a rental property.

Ultimately, we created a goal of purchasing more properties, building up our assets, and building up our revenue.

CHAPTER 8

Protect Your Future

Clason's Sixth Law:
Insure A Future Income

"The man who, because of his understanding of the laws
of wealth, acquireth a growing surplus, should give thought
to those future days."

– George Clason

Without exception, the best retirement plan is to start, build and expand your own business(es). That's not what we're taught, though, is it?

Like many, I was taught that the proper route to future security was to go to school, get good grades, get a safe and secure job, put some money in the stock market, build up enough savings to retire on, and hope that Social Security and or a pension provided enough money so that it all worked out for a comfortable living.

I learned pretty quickly how ridiculous that approach was. If I'd followed that advice, I would actually be working harder for a lower quality of life in my retirement years rather than the better quality of life I currently have and am on course for.

The best approach I have found is to build and expand a business.

Not just any business. You don't go about this thoughtlessly. You want to build a business where you can start small, and then develop skills, systems, or the people in the business so that it can grow into something big. Something that doesn't necessarily need you there to operate efficiently and effectively and generate revenue. One that could thrive and be successful even if you passed away.

This is the realization that hit me so hard when I went to that first seminar, back when my life was stalled and I knew I needed to make a change.

"My Lord," I remember thinking. "I've been doing it all wrong! I've been working for other people for thirteen years and I have very little to show for it!"

Yes, I had good experiences (and some not so good experiences) during those years. I gained some skills. I met some people. But can that be handed off to my son? Could I turn all of that hard work I'd poured into someone else's business into my own profit? Could I sell those thirteen years of effort and build my wealth?

You know I couldn't.

In fact, I was at the mercy of the company I worked for. They could downsize, move me across the country and/or fire me at any moment without me having any say in that process. I didn't have the wealth and I didn't have any control. I'd handed it all over to someone else to manage, only to hand it back to me piecemeal after I put in my time.

Even worse, the more money I made on sales and commissions, the more was taken out and given to Uncle Sam before I ever saw it. I was penalized for working harder for someone else by being put in a higher tax bracket and seeing even less money come my way.

That alternate path—building your own business instead of working for someone else—is one where income flows in and where business owners can spend their money on legitimate business expenses. It is only after that is spent that Uncle Sam taxes me on what is left. Essentially, you're allowed to build wealth quickly (and potentially faster) because you have more control over how you keep and spend your money before it's taxed.

This was mind-blowing to me.

The glaring difference between the two paths was only further clarified when I met people who had consistently built their own businesses over, say, eight years and had the things I wanted but was still lacking after thirteen years. They had purpose, they had a legacy that could be passed on to their children, and they had independence in their time and finances.

In eight years, they had it. In thirteen years, I was nowhere close.

I had to abandon that old model, and find a better approach. In my case, I found two.

Direct Sales Is Built On Success

The beauty of direct sales is that you can start small, on a part-time basis, and build the skills and connections you need to grow. You can take the time to learn to think differently (along the lines I've outlined in this book) about your approach to wealth. You can grow into what it takes to be a business owner.

And—this is the best part—you have free mentors.

Direct sales is unique in that it's an industry where people are enthusiastic not only about sharing, but also about caring and helping others find the path to independence. In most industries, you have to pay significant amounts to have access to this kind of mentorship.

Don't believe me?

When I started in real estate, I invested $24,000 in a mentor to teach me the business. (Note: invested, not paid—get the right mindset.) In my direct sales business, I invested $199 to start, and my mentors came with that for free!

Mentors are ready and waiting, in place to help you, in the direct sales industry. They want you to become your very best because your success is directly connected to their success. Everyone wins.

Real Estate Has Endless Options

Real estate has also proved to be an excellent way to secure income for your future.

My core business helped generate the cash that allowed me to start investing in real estate. In fact, I was only two years into my core business before I formed a second business specifically for real estate investments and holdings.

Historically, real estate has been one of the best retirement vehicles available because of its flexibility and endless options. You can purchase properties, hold onto them for echo cash flow, cash them out at the right price—whatever fits your retirement or current needs.

CHAPTER 9

Invest In Yourself

Seventh Law: Increase The Ability to Earn ("Invest in Ourselves")

"This is the process by which wealth is accumulated: first in small sums, then in larger ones as a man learns and becomes more capable."

– George Clason

Your ego can decimate your business and your wealth.

One of my mentors told me to never stop learning. She said that I should never allow my ego to convince me that I knew everything, that I'd arrived at peak knowledge. Since then, I've learned that if I want my wealth to become more, I must become more.

Jim Rohn, who had introduced me to George Clason's book initially, echoed this concept. "The problem with not wanting more is you won't have to become more," he said. "The book you won't read won't help."

Perhaps you've read the same articles I have, which repeatedly reveal that leaders are readers, that the most successful people in this world are always learning. I have made a practice of reading many, many books on a variety of topics, including not only business and finance, but also spirituality, leadership, health and wellness, race relations, economics, politics and social-psychology. At one point I was reading three books a week for over four months.

Why so many topics?

A well-read person is a well-rounded person. Reading books on narrow or limited topics puts blinders on you. Building wealth involves not only finances, but how to work with people, how to understand your own motivations, how to lead, and how to stay physically and spiritually healthy. Remember how I mentioned that it wasn't only important that you have financial intelligence, but emotional intelligence?

Success requires a broad spectrum of intelligence, or it is fleeting.

Do you want more in your life and your business? Do you want to know more to sustain that increase? That desire Rohn describes is crucial.

You don't have to read three books a week, but I encourage you to make a habit of reading on a schedule. You'll want to read a broad variety of books and topics that are going to help you improve yourself. Where do you want to be successful? What areas are you struggling with? Have you identified weak spots in your personal or financial dealings?

Read a book that answers those questions.

I also strongly encourage attending seminars, educational conferences or trainings in the field you want to become an expert in. You may even need to hire outside mentors or personal development coaches. These are all ways of investing in yourself. Remember when I said that you could rip away all the money from the wealthy and they'd have it back in no time? It's because you can take their money, but not their knowledge. Personally, my wife and I set aside thousands of dollars annually to attend conferences to continuously better ourselves. Investing back into yourself is highly crucial to building wealth.

Remember the old saying: the older I get, the more I realize I don't know anything.

Continuously educate yourself if you want to continuously earn.

CHAPTER 10

The Way Out

> *"Calm down. It's okay. I've been here before.*
> *I know how to get out."*
>
> – Unknown

If there's anything I want you to take away from this book, it's that it isn't about the numbers, but about the habits.

Know these laws. Consistently apply them. Make them a habit.

As Jim Rohn said to me, "Motivation is what gets you started. Habits are what keep you going."

Years ago, I was stuck in a hole. Mentally, physically, emotionally, spiritually, and certainly financially. This reminds me of one of my favorite poems by an unknown author.

An Addict Fell in a Hole

AN ADDICT FELL IN A HOLE and couldn't get out.

A businessman went by and the addict called out for help. The businessman threw him some money and told him to buy himself a ladder. But the addict could not buy a ladder in this hole he was in.

A doctor walked by. The addict said, "Help! I can't get out!" The doctor gave him some drugs and said, "Take this. It will relieve the pain." The addict said thanks, but when the pills ran out, he was still in the hole.

A well-known psychiatrist rode by and heard the addict's cries for help. He stopped and asked," How did you get there? Were you born there? Did your parents put you there? Tell me about yourself, it will alleviate your sense of loneliness." So the addict talked with him for an hour, then the psychiatrist had to leave, but he said he'd be back next week.

The addict thanked him, but he was still in the hole. A priest came by. The addict called for help. The priest gave him a Bible and said, "I'll say a prayer for you." He got down on his knees and prayed for the addict, then he left. The addict was very grateful, he read the Bible, but he was still stuck in the hole.

A recovering addict happened to be passing by. The addict cried out, "Hey, help me. I'm stuck in this hole!" Right away the recovering addict jumped down in the hole with him. The addict said, "What are you doing? Now we're both stuck here!!" But the recovering addict said, "Calm down. It's okay. I've been here before. I know how to get out."

"I know how to get out."

That line has stuck with me ever since I first read this poem because it's exactly how I feel.

I'm not just writing any of this book to write it. I'm not trying to give you something I don't possess. I'm *being for real* when I talk about living in that hole for basically my whole life.

Jamil Frazier is a recovering, financially-ignorant addict, just trying to help others like me out of this hole.

My greatest hope in sharing these principles is that you get started (or continue) on a path to controlling your finances, your life, and your retirement. It's your unique journey, but if I can do it with mine, I have no doubt you can do the same.

I want to see you living a life of complete abundance in every area, because you deserve to live the life of your dreams.

I'm rooting for you. And remember, keep it simple ... 10/10/10. Over time, watch what happens!

About Jamil Frazier

Jamil Frazier is a motivational speaker, author, certified health coach, personal development coach, and the founder and CEO of Think Life Is Different, Inc. Today, his coaching network has served over 50,000 clients and is growing—but his impact didn't always look this way.

In April 2012, he hit a pivotal moment where everything was out of balance. He was physically unhealthy, financially broken, relationally poor, and mentally frayed. Simply put, he was a mess. However, after deciding to build holistic health, he found traction on the path to true wealth.

Now he dedicates his life to guide individuals and organizations to achieve financial independence, healthy minds and bodies, and thriving relationships.

If there was only one thing he could do before leaving this earth, it would be to help people everywhere learn to think well. And he's just getting started.

For bookings, email: Jamil@ThinkLifeIsDifferent.com

Connect with Jamil:

⊚ | @therealjamilfrazier

▉ | facebook.com/thinklifeisdifferent

ThinkLifeIsDifferent.com

About Think Life Is Different, Inc.

Q: What is Think Life Is Different?

A: Think Life Is Different (TLID) is an educational, leadership development, and training company. It's where founder and CEO Jamil Frazier and his team work with individuals and organizations to achieve their goals and maximize potential. It's also where companies hire the TLID Speakers and trainers to speak, and where the TLID books, training courses, merchandise, and apparel are sold.

Q: How did the concept come about?

A: In April 2012, Jamil experienced a massive shift, charting a course for rapid personal change and evolution. With that growth he started experiencing life in a different way, from his conversations with his wife and patience as a father, to deepened humility and empathy with business partners, to his views on spirituality, money management, and personal development.

His dress, his hygiene, his standards, his expectations, his focus, his freedoms, and his options all changed. On days where he would have been working hard in medical sales, he was now walking the beach or in yoga classes. Everything changed, and this phrase was constantly on his lips, "Man ... and to think, life is so different."

While vacationing in Washington State, Jamil and his wife were leaving a beautiful home they'd rented for the week. While walking down the steps, he paused, realizing he would earn just a little less than half that day in echo income from enjoying life than he would've earned all month just years before while working fifty-plus hours per week.

At that moment, he shook his head and all he could say was, "think life is different."

Q: What is its mission?

A: To improve lives daily

Visit ThinkLifeIsDifferent.com for more ...

Get The Twelve Shifts

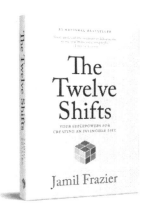

Did you know—you have twelve superpowers lying dormant within you, just waiting to be unlocked?

Maybe you've felt them deep inside you, telling you there's more to life. Maybe you've gotten stuck or hit a ceiling, and you don't know how to level up from where you are. Maybe you're tired of not living out your purpose—or you're not even sure what it is.

The Twelve Shifts is a step-by-step guide on how to unlock the 12 superpowers that will help you remove limits, crush barriers, smash through ceilings, afford anything, and become truly invincible. You'll reinvent your mindset, dig through the layers of grime your past has heaped on you, and reveal the superpowers to ensure nothing ever holds you back again.

You only have one life to live. Supercharge it by harnessing your mind's true power and unlocking the secret to more.

Join my insider's tribe to secure your copy of *The Twelve Shifts* at ThinkLifeIsDifferent.com.